A BUSINESS NOTION PUT IN MOTION

JIM WHITACRE, CPA

A BUSINESS NOTION PUT IN MOTION

THE WIT AND WISDOM OF
JIM WHITACRE

proving
press

This book is available at a bulk discount for educational purposes.
For bulk ordering, please contact info@columbuspublishinglab.com

Hardback ISBN: 978-1-63337-418-8
Paperback ISBN: 978-1-63337-416-4
E-book ISBN: 978-1-63337-417-1
LCCN: 2020914280

Book design and production by
Columbus Publishing Lab
47 N. 4th Street, Suite 204
Zanesville, OH 43701
www.columbuspublishinglab.com

Printed in the United States of America

FOREWORD

AS A YOUTH, JIM LOVED TO WRITE.

He published a humorous newspaper out of his home in Kansas City, MO. A friend of his contributed cartoon drawings. Born in 1915, Jim lived during the years when newspapers were thriving. He later wrote many poems for his wife, Marion, who he met while both were attending a business college in Kansas City.

Although he might have liked having a son, Jim was a wonderful father to his three daughters. Sue was born first, in 1941, and she was the apple of everyone's eye. When Jim joined the Army during World War II, he remained stateside and quickly returned to Sue's side when she contracted tonsillitis. Sue received one of the first penicillin shots, which saved her life.

When Sue was eight, some of her limelight was stolen by twin sisters, Joan and Jan. Jim proudly strolled his twin daughters past the wonderful statues in Kansas City's original Plaza area. As his daughters grew, Jim introduced them to stamp collecting, Erector sets, science projects, and baseball. He gathered the girls in the backyard to throw a baseball every night before dinner, when weather permitted. He was also the fearless parent who accompanied his daughters on scary rides at amusement parks.

Jim's character was so strong. He taught his children by example, never by lecturing. Treat others – <u>all others</u> – as you would like them to treat you. Serve your community. And always do your best.

Jim's love of writing was passed down to all three daughters, who either taught English or became editors and writers.

As one of the twins, I was especially proud that my dad's middle name (Graham) was also chosen as my middle name. Jim wrote a regular column entitled "Graham's Crackers, Rhyming Around" for the *Daily News* in Richardson, Texas.

Thanks for sharing your wit and wisdom, Dad. We're still chuckling.

Love,
Joan Graham Whitacre Harris

I HAVE A BUSINESS NOTION
THAT I THINK I WILL EXPLORE
IT'S BUYING CERTAIN ITEMS
AND THEN SELLING THEM FOR MORE

> I'LL KNOW WHAT ITEMS COST ME
> AND MY PRICES WILL BE FIRM
> WITH PROFITS PREDETERMINED
> ON A CASH-AND-CARRY TERM

I ALSO HAVE SOME MONEY
FOR AN INVENTORY STOCK
WITHOUT THE NEED TO BORROW
OR PLACE MY SHIRT IN HOCK

> THE MARKETPLACE IS READY
> AND THE CUSTOMERS ARE THERE
> IN SUFFICIENT NUMBER
> SO THAT I CAN GET A SHARE

SELLING DAILY ALL MY ITEMS
SHOULD PROVIDE ME WITH THE CASH
TO BUY FOR NEXT DAY'S BUSINESS
AND SOME PROFITS LEFT FOR HASH

I Plan to Sell Apples!

I HAD TO CHOOSE A CORNER
WHERE THE PEOPLE WOULD SLOW UP
WITH ROOM TO SEE MY APPLES
AND TO DROP COINS IN MY CUP

        I BOUGHT A CRATE OF APPLES
          AT A PRICE I COULD AFFORD
        SO NOT TO CREATE A SHORTAGE
      WHEN I PAID MY ROOM AND BOARD

MY FIRST SIGN JUST SAID "APPLES"
WHICH TURNED OUT TO BE REAL BAD
BECAUSE THE PEOPLE PASSING BY
COULD SEE CLEARLY WHAT I HAD

        I KNEW MY NEXT REQUIREMENT
         WAS TO MAKE ANOTHER SIGN
         WITH COLORS AND A SLOGAN
      LIKE "A HEALTHY WAY TO DINE"

MY NEW SALES ADVERTISING
WAS APPARENTLY WELL-PLANNED
MY CUP IS NOW A CASHBOX
AND MY CRATE BECAME A STAND

Telling Helps Selling

I SMILED AT ALL THE PEOPLE
WAITING FOR THE LIGHT TO CHANGE
AND SOON I HAD DEVELOPED
QUITE A CONVERSATION RANGE

I ALSO GATHERED KNOWLEDGE
OF THE KINDS OF WORK THEY DID
AND ACTED AS THEIR CHAPLAIN
WHEN A PROBLEM BLEW THEIR LID

ALTHOUGH I DID SOME TALKING
I DID NOT FORGET TO SELL
AND DEVELOPED SEVERAL TACTICS
THAT WOULD HELP ME TO DO WELL

I EVEN POLISHED APPLES
SO THEIR SURFACE REALLY SHOWN
BUT REALIZED THAT SELLING
COULDN'T COME FROM THIS ALONE

All That Glitters Isn't Sold

BY NOW I'VE BEEN IN BUSINESS
A SUFFICIENT TIME TO KNOW
THAT I'LL NEED SOME ASSISTANTS
IF I EVER WANT TO GROW

        I'LL LOOK FOR FRIENDLY PEOPLE
        WHO WILL HAVE A WORKING PRIDE
        AND HAVE SOME SKILLS TO OFFER
        THAT THEY'RE NOT INCLINED TO HIDE

I'LL PUT THEM ON SOME CORNERS
AND IN BUSINESS BUILDINGS TOO,
PROVIDE THEM WITH THE APPLES
AND HOPE THEY SELL A FEW

        THEY ALSO MUST LIKE APPLES
        AND BELIEVE WHAT PEOPLE SAY
        ABOUT A DAILY APPLE
        KEEPING DOCTORS FAR AWAY

FOR THOSE WHO ARE GOOD WORKERS
AND WHOSE BUSINESS VOLUME JUMPS
I'LL SHARE WITH THEM MY PROFITS
BUT THE OTHERS WILL GET LUMPS

To Share Is Fair

I'LL VISIT EACH LOCATION
TO LET THE SALES FOLKS KNOW
THAT TEAMWORK IS IMPORTANT
IN ASSISTING US TO GROW

        I'LL CONCENTRATE ON TRAINING
        'TIL MY PEOPLE HAVE ADVANCED
        IN BUSINESS UNDERSTANDING
        AND THEIR CONFIDENCE ENHANCED

AND SHARING ALL MY TACTICS
PLUS MY CONVERSATION BASE
CAN HELP THEM WITH THEIR ACTIONS
WHEN THEY'RE SELLING FACE-TO-FACE

        I'M TOLD THAT INSPIRATION
        NEEDS SOME DOLLARS TO GET HOT
        SO I ARRANGED A BONUS
        FOR THE MONTHLY LEADING SPOT

AND SINCE WE'RE MEETING PEOPLE
WHO ARE NORMALLY WELL-DRESSED
I'M INSISTING THAT MY SALES FOLKS
ALWAYS KEEP THEIR CLOTHES WELL-PRESSED

Let People See
We're Wrinkle-free

I'M RECEIVING PURCHASE DISCOUNTS
FOR THE VOLUME THAT I BUY
AND WITH THIS ADDED INCOME
I MAY START TO WEAR A TIE

                    AND IF I LIMIT SPENDING
                      SO MY CASH ACCUMULATES
                I'LL START A PLAN FOR SAVING
             THAT WILL PAY GOOD INTEREST RATES

I'LL PATRONIZE THE BANKERS
WHO BUY APPLES EVERY DAY
TO SHOW THEM THAT MY METHODS
HAVE MADE BUSINESS REALLY PAY

                   AND WHEN THEY LOOK IN WONDER
                     AT MY GROWING SAVINGS PLAN
                       I MAY BECOME RESPECTED
                     AS A SKILLFUL BUSINESSMAN

I'll Look Good
as Bosses Should

MY PEOPLE HAVE BEEN ASKING
FOR A WAY TO EARN MORE CASH
SO THEY'D BE EATING BETTER
THAN THEIR DAILY PLATES OF HASH

I UNDERSTAND THEIR WISHES
SINCE THEY COINCIDE WITH MINE
AND SO WILL DO SOME THINKING
ON A BETTER WAY TO DINE

WE HAD A FEW SHORT MEETINGS
DURING TIMES WHEN IT WAS RAINING
AND DECIDED WE WERE READY
FOR A CHANCE TO USE OUR TRAINING

WE'LL BE EXPANSION MINDED
AND WILL PLAN SOME WORK TO DO
THAT CAN PROVIDE A CHALLENGE
AND INCREASE INCOME TOO

SINCE ALL OUR APPLE SALES FOLKS
COULD BE CLASSED AMONG THE BEST
WE FELT THIS GROUP OF TALENTS
COULD SURVIVE MOST ANY TEST

In the Mood
for Better Food

OUR PLAN DEVELOPED QUICKLY
BUT WE KEPT OUR POWDER DRY
WITH COMMON SENSE PREVAILING
SINCE EXCITEMENT WAS SO HIGH

AT FIRST WE'LL NEED SOME FUNDING
FROM A LOCAL BANKING SOURCE
TO BUY THE RIGHT EQUIPMENT
AND TO PAY OUR WORKING FORCE

WE'LL TELL THEM WHAT WE'RE PLANNING
AND WHAT PROSPECTS LIE AHEAD
THAT WILL ASSURE REPAYMENT
ON A SCHEDULED PAYMENT SPREAD

WE'LL RENT AN EMPTY BUILDING
FOR OUR FIRST PRODUCTION LINES
AND START OUR ADVERTISING
BY ARRANGING FOR SOME SIGNS

WE'LL HIRE A PRODUCT EXPERT
WHO'LL BE OUR INSIDE COACH
WHILE WE CONTACT THE MARKET
WITH A STRATEGICAL APPROACH

We Plan to Try
for Apple Pie

WE VISITED SOME BAKERIES
ON THEIR OPEN TOURING DAYS
BUT KEPT OUR PURPOSE HIDDEN
WHILE OBSERVING ALL THEIR WAYS

ALTHOUGH WE KNOW OUR APPLES,
MAKING PIE DOUGH WILL BE NEW
SO WE HOPE THAT OUR BAKERS
LEARN EXACTLY WHAT TO DO

WE BOUGHT EACH ONE AN APRON
AND SOME FANCY ROLLING PINS
INSTALLED SOME BAKING OVENS
AND PUT FLOUR IN THE BINS

WE IMPROVISED SOME CUTTERS
SO THE APPLES COULD BE SLICED
AND OBTAINED EXOTIC POWDERS
SO THE PIES WOULD BE WELL-SPICED

OUR EXPERT COACHED THE OTHERS
'TIL HIS FACE WAS TURNING BLUE
BUT SOON THEY WERE PRODUCING
JUST AS WELL AS HE COULD DO

Taking to Baking

WE HAD AN EARLY PROBLEM
THAT WAS CAUSING CONSTERNATION
WHEN BURN-CLAIMS BY OUR BAKERS
RAISED OUR WORKMEN'S COMPENSATION

THEY TOLD US THAT OUR OVENS
HAD TO STAY SO VERY HOT
THAT EVEN BEING CAREFUL
COULDN'T STOP THE BURNS THEY GOT

WE EXAMINED ALL EQUIPMENT
JUST IN CASE IT WAS TO BLAME
AND CHECKED THE INSULATION
FOR PROTECTION FROM THE FLAME

WE DIDN'T FIND ONE PROBLEM
THAT DIRECTLY WOULD RELATE
TO ACCIDENTS THAT HAPPENED
AND OUR HIGH INSURANCE RATE

OUR SYMPATHETIC AGENT
WHOM WE CALLED IN TO ADVISE
SAID HE HAD NOTICED BAKERS
STICKING FINGERS IN THE PIES

Painful Sensations from Burning Temptations

WE SET UP SAFETY STANDARDS
AND SOME FIRE PREVENTION TOOLS
AND EMPHASIZED TO BAKERS
THE IMPORTANCE OF THESE RULES

THEY AREN'T TO TASTE THEIR BAKING
WHETHER IT IS HOT OR COLD
AND KEEP THEIR FEET OFF THE TABLES
WHERE THE DOUGH IS BEING ROLLED

DEBRIS FOUND IN THE HALLWAYS
IS TO BE PICKED UP ON SIGHT
AND IF IT IS TOO HEAVY
THEY'RE TO PAINT IT GREEN OR WHITE

ALTHOUGH OUR RULES HAD LOGIC
THEY PRODUCED A LOT OF FLAK
AND MANY OF OUR WORKERS
SAID THEIR ARMY DAYS WERE BACK

Rules for GI's
Are Good for Pies

BUT BAKERS STILL GOT BLISTERS
MUCH MORE OFTEN THAN THEY SHOULD
ALTHOUGH PREVENTIVE MEASURES
WERE INSTALLED AS BEST WE COULD

WE USED A LOT OF STORAGE
JUST TO KEEP BAND-AIDS SUPPLIED
AND NURSES WERE SO BUSY
THAT THEY COULDN'T STEP OUTSIDE

SINCE ABSENCES WERE FREQUENT
FROM OUR PLANT PRODUCTION LINE
WE CONTINUED OBSERVATIONS
FOR WHAT ELSE WE COULD REFINE

IT SOON BECAME APPARENT
THAT SOME BURNS WERE RATHER SMALL
AND FREQUENTLY WE DOUBTED
FOLKS WERE REALLY BURNED AT ALL

SO THEN WE FOUND THE REASON
FOR OUR PIE PRODUCTION WOES
AND CHANGED OUR STAFF OF NURSES
FROM YOUNG LOVELIES TO OLD PROS

```
┌─────────────────────────────────────┐
│                                     │
│         This Stalls                 │
│         Sick Calls                  │
│                                     │
└─────────────────────────────────────┘
```

This Stalls
Sick Calls

WE NOTICED IN OUR SURVEYS
THAT OUR WORKERS DIDN'T CARE
ABOUT THEIR OWN APPEARANCE
AND THE BAKING ROOMS THEY SHARE

SINCE WE EXPECTED VISITS
OF SOME PEOPLE FROM OUTSIDE
OUR PLANT MUST LOOK MUCH NEATER
AND OUR WORKERS SHOULDN'T HIDE

WE SET UP CLEANING SCHEDULES
FOR EACH WORKING GROUP TO USE
AND TOLD THEM TO WEAR APRONS
AND TO ALWAYS WEAR SOME SHOES

WE ALSO HAD A PROBLEM
WITH SOME WORKERS AND THEIR HAIR
BECAUSE IT MUST BE COVERED
BY THE BAKER'S CAPS THEY WEAR

SO WE PROVIDED CHOICES
FOR THOSE GUYS WITH LONG HAIR STYLES
THEY COULD WEAR FOOTBALL HELMETS
OR GET HAIR CUTS WITH A SMILE

We Now Have an
Unsmiling Football Team

ALTHOUGH WE'RE MAKING PROFITS
AND OUR PRODUCT'S SELLING WELL
WE STILL DEPEND ON OTHERS
TO DISTRIBUTE WHAT WE SELL

REGARDLESS OF THEIR SCHEDULES
THERE ARE TIMES WHEN THEY DELAY
AND UPSET OUR ACCOUNTANTS
WHEN THE CUSTOMERS WON'T PAY

AN OBVIOUS IMPROVEMENT
WOULD BE JUST TO HELP OURSELVES
BY MAKING QUICK DELIVERIES
FROM THE FRESH STOCK ON OUR SHELVES

SO BACK TO FRIENDLY BANKERS
FOR SOME MONEY AND ADVICE
AND NEGOTIATED CREDIT
BASED ON AN ESTIMATED PRICE

WE STARTED CHECKING DEALERS
TO GET PRICES FOR OUR FLEET
AND FOUND SUCH COMPETITION
THAT OUR ESTIMATES WERE BEAT

Deals for Wheels

WE WEREN'T SURE HOW TO MANAGE
ALL THE TRUCKS AND DRIVERS TOO
SO NOW WE'VE HIRED A FOREMAN
WHO WILL KNOW JUST WHAT TO DO

WE HOPE HE SOLVES ALL PROBLEMS
WITH OUR NEW DELIVERY FLEET
AND TRIES TO KEEP 'EM ROLLING
SO THEY WON'T CLOG UP THE STREET

WE'LL START COMMUNICATIONS
WHICH TRADITION MAY PRECLUDE
WHEN THOSE WHO TAKE THE ORDERS
SPEAK TO THOSE WHO BAKE THE FOOD

WE'LL ALSO NEED GOOD SCHEDULES
AND CONTROLLING OF OUR STOCK
TO COORDINATE OUR ORDERS
AND DELIVERIES BY THE CLOCK

AND BAKING WILL NEED TIMING
SO THAT PIES ARE AT THE DOOR
WHEN TRUCKS ARRIVE FOR LOADING
BUT NOT VERY LONG BEFORE

Fresh Pie Loads
on All the Roads

THIS SURFACE TRANSPORTATION
HAS MORE HEADACHES THAN WE THOUGHT
IT SEEMS THAT PRESENT SCHEDULES
TAKE MORE TRUCKS THAN WE HAVE BOUGHT

WE KNOW WE CALCULATED
ALL REQUIREMENTS WE COULD FIND
AND YET OUR WEEK'S DELIVERIES
WOUND UP TWO FULL DAYS BEHIND

WE TESTED ALL ROUTE SCHEDULES
AND THE VOLUME EACH WOULD TAKE
BUT WHEN WE CHECKED THE DRIVERS
FOUND THEY COULDN'T STAY AWAKE

THEY SAID THEIR NIGHTLY SLUMBERS
WERE ENOUGH TO LAST ALL DAY
AND YET WHEN LUNCH WAS OVER
THEY FELT SLEEPY RIGHT AWAY

WE SOON FOUND OUT THE ANSWER
WAS THEY ATE MORE THAN THEY SHOULD
(WHICH GAVE US MIXED EMOTIONS
SINCE THEY SAID OUR PIES WERE GOOD)

Good Dessert
Shouldn't Hurt

OUR ADDED BUSINESS FUNCTIONS
HAVE ALREADY INCREASED SALES
BUT SAVINGS ON DELIVERIES
ARE NOT FILLING PROFIT PAILS

WE'RE THINKING OF EXPANSION
BUT MUST CERTAINLY BE SURE
OUR PRESENT BUSINESS VENTURE
WILL CONTINUE TO ENDURE

IF WE CAN USE OUR PEOPLE
AND OUR OWN FACILITIES
WE WON'T NEED MORE INVESTMENTS
AND CAN STILL EXPAND WITH EASE

WE MUST ASSURE THIS PRODUCT
IS AS GOOD AS NUMBER ONE
AND CONTRIBUTES TO OUR PROFITS
WHICH I SHARE WITH EVERYONE

OUR CUSTOMERS ARE HAPPY
AND MUST THINK OUR PRODUCT'S FINE
SO WITH THIS REPUTATION
WE WILL JUST ADD TO OUR LINE

Now to Try
Some Cherry Pie

ANNOUNCEMENTS OF OUR CHERRY PIE
WERE MADE A NOVEL WAY
AND PLANNED TO HIT THE PUBLIC
ON G. WASHINGTON'S BIRTHDAY

                    OUR ADVERTISING AGENT
                    HAD US BOX 5,000 PIES
          AND SHIP THEM TO SOME AIRPORTS
              FOR DELIVERY FROM THE SKIES

A CONTRACT FOR SOME AIRPLANES
WAS ARRANGED IN EVERY STATE
AND PARACHUTES WERE FURNISHED
THAT WOULD CARRY THE PIE WEIGHT

          WE PLACED IN EACH OF THE BOXES
               A REQUEST FOR PROMPT REPLY
          FROM THOSE WHO ATE THE CONTENTS
               AS TO HOW THEY LIKED THE PIE

THE PIE-DROP WAS SUCCESSFUL
AND REPLIES WERE VERY GOOD
EXCEPT FOR ONE CAR OWNER
WHO HAD PIE SPLASHED ON HIS HOOD

A Splashy Ad
Can't Be All Bad

WE DID SEND AIR FREIGHT SHIPMENTS
BUT TOO MUCH TIME EXPIRED
FROM AIRPLANES TO THE TABLES
WHERE GOOD PIE TASTE WAS REQUIRED

                    WE REALIZED OUR ERROR
          WHEN WE SKY-DROPPED ALL THOSE PIES
                  BECAUSE WE HADN'T FOLLOWED
              WITH SOME COUNTRY-WIDE SUPPLIES

OUR PROFITS ALSO SUFFERED
WHEN WE SHIPPED TO MANY STATIONS
AND COULDN'T INCREASE PRICES
UNDER PHASE IV LIMITATIONS

                    SO ALL THAT ADVERTISING
                  PROVED OF LITTLE BENEFIT
               EXCEPT TO THOSE FEW PERSONS
              WHO WERE NEAR A PIE-DROP HIT

Without a Doubt
We Should Phase Out

WE ALSO FOUND SOME PROBLEMS
IN OUR CHERRY PREPARATION
THAT WEREN'T ANTICIPATED
WHEN WE FORMED THE OPERATION

                MACHINES FOR SLICING APPLES
                 HAD BEEN ALTERED JUST A BIT
           SO THEY COULD CLEAN THE CHERRIES
                 AND REMOVE EACH CHERRY PIT

OUR REDESIGN WAS FAULTY
SINCE WE SOMEHOW FAILED TO GUESS
THAT HANDLING SOFTER CHERRIES
COULD RESULT IN QUITE A MESS

             CONTAINERS FOR SLICED APPLES
            WERE CONSTRUCTED RATHER LOOSE
                 SO WHEN WE PUT IN CHERRIES
              THEY WOULD NOT RETAIN THE JUICE

IT SEEMS A WASTEFUL PRACTICE
TO KEEP WASHING JUICE AWAY—
WE NEED SOME WAY TO USE IT
(AS ECOLOGISTS WOULD SAY)

A Solution
for Pollution

OF COURSE OUR FIRST OBJECTIVE
WAS TO KEEP THE PLANT FLOOR CLEAN
BY KEEPING JUICE FROM DRIPPING
OFF EACH TABLE AND MACHINE

WE PLACED A GLASS CONTAINER
EVERY PLACE THE JUICE COULD GO
BUT THEN HAD TO BE CAREFUL
THAT THESE DIDN'T OVERFLOW

WE STILL WERE FACING A CHALLENGE
TO FIND OTHER USES FOR
THE JUICE WE'D BE COLLECTING
AND NOT WASTING ANYMORE

WE CALLED IN A CONSULTANT
AND EXPLAINED THE JUICE WAS FREE
AND IF IT COULD BE BOTTLED
WE'D HAVE PRODUCT NUMBER THREE

SINCE MANY HAVE A BREAKFAST
THAT INCLUDES A GLASS OF JUICE
WE TRIED OURS—AND WE LIKED IT
SO WE KNEW IT HAD ONE USE

Now Turn Us Loose with Cherry Juice

OUR SALES ACCOUNTING FIGURES
SHOW ALL PRODUCTS SELLING WELL
EVEN OUR LATEST VENTURE
IS REALLY DOING SWELL

WE'RE HAPPY WITH THIS INCREASE
EVEN THOUGH IT STARTED SLOW
WITH LARGE ACCUMULATIONS
BEFORE SALES BEGAN TO GROW

WE ASKED PRODUCTION PEOPLE
WHETHER THEY COULD TELL US WHY
THE CHERRY JUICE IN BOTTLES
SOLD MUCH BETTER THAN OUR PIE

THEIR ANSWER WAS SO SHOCKING
THAT WE ALMOST CLIMBED THE WALL
IT SEEMS OUR JUICE FERMENTED
AND DEVELOPED ALCOHOL

NO WONDER THAT THE ORDERS
FOR THIS PRODUCT HAD GROWN BIG
AND CUSTOMERS STAYED HAPPY
WHEN THEY HAD OUR JUICE TO SWIG

Hold the Line
for Cherry Wine

BUT ONCE THE SHOCK WAS OVER
AND WE ANALYZED OUR PLIGHT
IT SOON BECAME APPARENT
THAT WE COULD BE IN A FIGHT

                GOOD CUSTOMERS WERE FLOCKING
          TO THE STORES THAT SOLD OUR STUFF
                 SO IF WE STOPPED PRODUCTION
          THE STORE OWNERS MIGHT GET TOUGH

AND YET OUR BUSINESS MORALS
WOULDN'T EVEN LET US STALL
BECAUSE WE HAD NO LICENSE
FOR PRODUCING ALCOHOL

                    WE SENT OUT MANY LETTERS
                         IN APOLOGETIC STYLE
                  THAT SAID OUR CORPORATION
                     WAS IN JEOPARDY A WHILE

WE CALLED BACK UNSOLD BOTTLES
WHILE WE EMPTIED TANKS TO NIL
AND HOPED THE "REVENOOERS"
WOULDN'T THINK WE HAD A STILL

We Know That Stills Belong in Hills

WE SOLD THE LIQUID PROCESS
FOR A FRACTION OF ITS COST
AND FIGURED ALL EXPENSES
PLUS OUR OWN HARD WORK WAS LOST

      WE DID KEEP THOSE CONTAINERS
      SO THE JUICES WOULDN'T SPREAD
      BUT WITHOUT OFFSET INCOME
      THESE JUST INCREASED OVERHEAD

WE STILL GOT NASTY LETTERS
FROM THE FOLKS WHO LIKED OUR JUICE
BUT STUCK TO OUR DECISIONS
WHICH HAD KEPT US FROM THE NOOSE

      SOME SAID WE SHOULD BE LICENSED
      SINCE OUR DRINK WAS VERY GOOD
      BUT WE SAID THAT OUR CHARTER
      DIDN'T INDICATE WE COULD

WE CHALKED UP OUR ADVENTURE
TO OUR BUSINESS LEARNING CURVE
AND PROMISED ALL OUR PEOPLE
THAT WE HADN'T LOST OUR NERVE

To Stay on Curve
Will Take Some Nerve

WE NOW SEEM TOO COMPLACENT
FOR CONTINUING SUCCESS
AND WITH OUR COMPETITION
WE MAY SOON BE SELLING LESS

AGAIN WE STARTED PLANNING
TO DEVELOP SOMETHING WISE
IN LINE WITH OUR SUCCESSES
WE'VE ACHIEVED IN MAKING PIES

OUR BRAINSTORMING WAS HEAVY
AND THE IDEAS WERE KNEE-DEEP
BUT AS WE CHECKED THE DETAILS
THERE WERE NONE THAT WE COULD KEEP

WE TRIED TO FIND SOME READING
THAT COULD GIVE US A NEW LOOK
BUT FOUND THAT REAL ACHIEVERS
HAD NO TIME TO WRITE A BOOK

WE'RE NOW IN YELLOW PAGES
LOOKING FOR A FIRM TO BUY
WHOSE PRODUCTS ARE SUCCESSFUL
AND RELATED TO A PIE

It Seems Wise
to Stay with Pies

A CANDIDATE FOR PURCHASE
WAS DISCOVERED DOWN THE STREET
WITH PRODUCTS WELL-ACCEPTED
AND WITH QUALITY COMPLETE

                    IT WILL BE SOME DIVERSION
                FROM OUR PRESENT LINE OF PIES
                   BUT HAS INVOLVED OUR BAKING
                    AS A PART OF OUR SUPPLIES

WE MADE AN EARLY VISIT
TO OBSERVE THIS CANDIDATE
AND TOLD THE PRESENT OWNERS
THAT THEIR PRODUCTS HAD BEEN GREAT

            THEY SAID THEY'D HAD GOOD BUSINESS
              SINCE THE FIRST YEAR THEY'D BEGUN
                     AND HAD MADE SO MUCH MONEY
                 THEY WERE READY FOR SOME FUN

SO, ON THIS HAPPY BASIS
AND THE INTEREST THAT WE HAD
THE PRICE WAS SETTLED QUICKLY
FOR WHICH ALL OF US WERE GLAD

Some New Plans
for Tin Pie Pans

OUR LAWYERS DID INFORM US
THAT WE SHOULD INCORPORATE
TO KEEP THIS ACQUISITION
WITHIN ALL RULES OF STATE

      THIS WAS SOMEWHAT SURPRISING
      SINCE WE'D FAILED TO REALIZE
        OUR BUSINESS WAS MATURING
         TO A PUBLIC INTEREST SIZE

SO FROM A SINGLE OWNER
TO A CORPORATE MODE
WILL LET ME CHANGE MY TITLE
AND HAVE MORE TO SHARE MY LOAD

      WE'LL CHART OFFICIAL DUTIES
        WITH AUTHORITIES TO MATCH
       AND ORGANIZE THE STRUCTURE
      SO IT WON'T REQUIRE A PATCH

WE'LL LIST OUR STOCK FOR ISSUE
AND EXCEPT FOR WHAT I OWN
GIVE OPTIONS TO OUR PEOPLE
AND THEN SELL THE REST BY PHONE

Fill the Sock
with Common Stock

WE NOW HAVE MANY OWNERS
EVEN THOUGH I'M STILL IN CHARGE
INCLUDING THOSE FINE PEOPLE
WHO HAD HELPED US GROW SO LARGE

OUR FINANCE INFORMATION
IS NOW FORMALLY ANNOUNCED
AND OPERATING DETAILS
ARE BECOMING MORE PRONOUNCED

OUR VISITORS ARE HAPPY
WITH MOST EVERYTHING THEY SEE
INCLUDING OUR FINE PEOPLE
AND HOPEFULLY WITH ME

BUT NOW WE'RE BEING PRESSURED
SINCE WE HAVE SOME CASH ON HAND
TO UP THE CORPORATION
SO IT'S KNOWN THROUGHOUT THE LAND

NOW WE'RE BACK TO PLANNING
AND (WE HOPE) ARE WISER TOO
AND WON'T START ANY ACTIONS
THAT WE CANNOT FOLLOW THROUGH

Try to Boast
from Coast to Coast

OUR RECENT ADVERTISING
TO A NATIONWIDE EXTENT
PROVED THIS WAS POINTLESS SELLING
IF NO PIES WERE EVER SENT

WE COULD SET UP MORE PLACES
WHERE OUR PRODUCTS COULD BE MADE
AND DELIVERED TO CONSUMERS
SO THE FRESHNESS WOULDN'T FADE

BUT WE WOULD NEED AN EXPERT
IN EACH PLANT THAT WE DESIGNED
TO ASCERTAIN WHETHER PRODUCTION
KEPT OUR QUALITY IN MIND

WE DO HAVE MANY EXPERTS
ON OUR CURRENT FACTORY TEAM
BUT IF SOME TRANSFERRED ELSEWHERE
WE WOULD LOSE OUR GROUP ESTEEM

WE'D LIKE TO HAVE AN ANSWER
THAT WOULD KEEP OUR GROUP ON HAND
AND STILL PROVIDE EXPANSION
THAT OUR SHAREHOLDERS DEMAND

Togetherness
Will Sure Impress

OUR MEETINGS WEREN'T PRODUCING
ANY PLANS THAT WE COULD USE
THAT HAD NO HIGH-RISK FACTORS
OR NO PROSPECTS WE COULD LOSE

WE THEN CHECKED OTHER BAKERIES
TO SEE HOW WE COULD RELATE
OUR DISTRIBUTION PROBLEMS
TO THEIR SELLING OUT OF STATE

IT SEEMS THAT BAKERY PRODUCTS
MUST BE FROZEN OR WELL-WRAPPED
TO REACH THE NATION'S MARKETS
WITH SUFFICIENT FLAVOR TRAPPED

AND THOSE WHO SELL FRESH BAKING
WITH A QUALITY THAT'S GOOD
SEEMED GENERALLY TO COVER
JUST THEIR LOCAL NEIGHBORHOOD

SINCE MANY SHARE OUR PROBLEM
WE HAVE FINALLY RESOLVED
IT WILL TAKE PIONEERING
IF IT'S EVER TO BE SOLVED

We Must Be Near a New Frontier

OUR SEARCH HAD NOT UNCOVERED
A SOLUTION WE COULD SEE
BUT THANKS TO ALL OUR TRAVELS
WE PERHAPS HAVE FOUND THE KEY

THE FOOD SERVED ON AIRPLANES
WAS AS TASTY AS COULD BE
INCLUDING DESSERT ITEMS
IN A WIDE VARIETY

WE STUDIED FLYING SCHEDULES
AND CONCLUDED THAT THIS MEANT
OUR PIES COULD KEEP THEIR FRESHNESS
REGARDLESS OF WHERE THEY WENT

WE KNEW THAT FASTER SHIPPING
WOULD BE BASED ON AIRCRAFT SPEED
BUT ONLY COST REDUCTION
WOULD GIVE PROFITS THAT WE NEED

DISCUSSIONS WITH SOME EXPERTS
FINALLY SHOWED US WHAT TO TRY
IN FINALIZING CONTRACTS
WITH THE FOLKS WHO RIDE THE SKY

An Unusual Try
for Pie in the Sky

WE'LL SHARE JOINT ADVERTISING
THAT WILL MENTION BOTH OF US
AND THEY'LL HELP PIE DELIVERIES
WHERE THEY HAVE A TRUCK OR BUS

                    COORDINATED SCHEDULES
                SHOULD PREVENT A BAD DELAY
            AND MOISTURE-PROOF CONTAINERS
          SHOULD KEEP PIES FRESH ALL THE WAY

WE DON'T KNOW JUST HOW NOVEL
THESE ARRANGEMENTS MAY HAVE SEEMED
BUT WE ACHIEVED OBJECTIVES
EVEN BETTER THAN WE DREAMED

                OUR PIES WERE WELL-ACCEPTED
              AND COMPLAINTS WERE VERY FEW
              FROM PASSENGERS ON AIRPLANES
                OR THEIR HOSTESSES AND CREW

OUR COST INCREASE WAS MINOR
SO OUR PROFITS STAYED INTACT
AND PLANS TO "UP" THE BUSINESS
HAVE BY NOW BECOME A FACT

Joint Operations Help Public Relations

HAVING SOLVED THESE PROBLEMS
WILL NOW GIVE US TIME TO SEE
IF OUR FINANCIAL DATA
IS AS GOOD AS IT CAN BE

WE STILL ARE KEEPING RECORDS
IN THE RATHER SIMPLE WAYS
THAT WE HAD STARTED USING
IN OUR EARLY BUSINESS DAYS

WE HIRED SOME SYSTEMS PEOPLE
AND PROVIDED THEM THE CHORE
OF MODERNIZING RECORDS
SO REPORTS COULD TELL US MORE

THEY SAID OUR PRESENT METHODS
HAD TO BE COMPUTERIZED
SO WE'D HAVE TIMELY DATA
AND WOULD NEVER BE SURPRISED

WE RENTED A COMPUTER
AND SOME NEW PERIPHERALS
INCLUDING OPTIC READERS
AND SOME VERY PRETTY GIRLS

Systems Are Beauties
When Run by Some Cuties

OUR SYSTEMS STARTED FILLING
ALL OUR INFORMATION NEEDS
AND ALL THE SYSTEMS PEOPLE
RECEIVED CREDIT FOR THEIR DEEDS

        BUT MANAGERS HAD TROUBLE
        WITH THE FAST REPORTING GAME
        AND RARELY EVER FINISHED
        BY THE TIME THE NEXT BATCH CAME

AND WITH OUR FAST COMPUTER
THERE WAS SURPLUS TIME EACH DAY
SO SYSTEMS PEOPLE HANKERED
FOR MORE PROGRAMS THEY COULD PLAY

        THEY SOON HAD AUTOMATED
        MOST DECISIONS EVERYWHERE
        AND EVEN MY OWN OFFICE
        COULD BE RUN WITHOUT ME THERE

THIS DIDN'T HELP MY EGO
AND MY PRIDE WAS SOMEWHAT BENT
TO THINK THAT A COMPUTER
COULD REPLACE THE PRESIDENT

Can't Disagree with EDP[1]

AFTER AUTOMATING PEOPLE
WITHIN ALL THE OFFICE GROUPS
THE SYTEMS EXPERTS HEADED
TOWARD OUR OWN PRODUCTION TROOPS

          THEY SAW OUR MANUAL PROCESS
        AND THE ROUTINE SKILLS REQUIRED
       AND SAID A RUBE NAMED GOLDBERG
      WOULD HAVE REALLY BEEN INSPIRED

WE REDESIGNED EQUIPMENT
FOR COMPUTER INTERFACE
AND AFTER SOME DEBUGGING
THE NEW SYSTEM WAS IN PLACE

          WE SENT OUR SKILLFUL BAKERS
          ON VACATIONS THEY WERE DUE
       AND WATCHED THE PIE PRODUCTION
         AS ITS OUTPUT REALLY GREW

BUT SALESMEN STARTED GRUMBLING
THAT THEY SOON WOULD BE IN DUTCH
IF ALL OUR TASTY PRODUCTS
LOST THEIR QUALITY SO MUCH

We Might Need to Try for Dutch Apple Pie

OUR QUALITY REDUCTION
WAS CONFIRMED BY OUR OWN TEST
AND ALSO BY CONSUMERS
WHO HAD THOUGHT OUR PIES WERE BEST

    THE DESIGNERS OF OUR SYSTEM
    CLAIMED THERE WAS NO BIG MISTAKE
    AND SAID THEY'D USED THE JUDGMENTS
    THAT OUR BAKERS USUALLY MAKE

WE ASKED AN EXPERT BAKER
TO COME IN FOR A REVIEW
OF ALL THIS PROCESS LOGIC
AND THE AUTOMATION TOO

    HE SAID THE SYSTEMS THEORY
    HAD A LOT OF PAPER FRILLS
    THAT WHEN APPLIED TO BAKING
    COULDN'T MATCH THE BAKER'S SKILLS

AND REGARDLESS OF THE TEMPO
THAT OUR PRODUCT LINES DISPLAYED
OUR PIES WOULD NOT BE TASTY
UNLESS SKILLFULLY HAND-MADE

Too Much Haste
Affects the Taste

WE REPORTED TO DIRECTORS
ALL THE FACTS WE COULD DEFINE
AND SAID OUR COST REDUCTION
HAD INSTEAD CAUSED SALES DECLINE

      WE CHARTED TRENDS AND NUMBERS
        BUT NO MATTER HOW WE TRIED
        THE DECREASE IN OUR PROFITS
        WAS A FACT WE COULDN'T HIDE

THEY QUESTIONED OUR DECISIONS
AND OUR INFORMATION BASE
SO THEY COULD FACE SHAREHOLDERS
AT THE ANNUAL MEETING PLACE

      WE TRIED TO OFFER REASONS
      THAT WOULD JUSTIFY OUR ACTS
      BUT FAILED TO SOUND CONVINCING
      IN RELATION TO THE FACTS

WE KNOW THAT THIS DISASTER
HAS EXTRACTED HEAVY TOLL
BUT HOPE OUR NEW SHAREHOLDERS
WON'T INSIST THAT HEADS SHOULD ROLL

Just One More Chance to Show Advance

THERE WAS MUCH CRITICISM
OF DECISION MANAGEMENT
BUT PROMISING IMPROVEMENT
I REMAINED AS PRESIDENT

                    I ALSO KEPT MY PEOPLE
          EVEN THOUGH THEY WERE DOWNCAST
               AND TRIED TO START REACTIONS
            SO THE PROBLEMS WOULDN'T LAST

WE DID PLAN ONE CORRECTION
WHICH DIRECTORS THEN APPROVED
TO STOP THE AUTOMATION
AND HAVE ALL ITS PARTS REMOVED

               DISMANTLING COSTS WERE HEAVY
          AND OUR PLANT WAS CLOSED A WHILE
             WHICH COUPLED WITH NO SELLING
               MADE IT REALLY HARD TO SMILE

WE CALLED BACK ALL OUR BAKERS
TO RESTORE PRODUCTION LINES
AND SENT OUR SYSTEMS PEOPLE
QUICKLY TO THE OLD SALT MINES

It's Hard to Fault Their Mining Salt

WE DID OFFSET SOME LOSSES
WITH OUR OLD EQUIPMENT SALES
BUT NOTICED THAT ACCOUNTANTS
WERE STILL CHEWING ON THEIR NAILS

THEY'RE TRYING TO ASSEMBLE
ALL THE AUTOMATION COST
INCLUDING RESTORATIONS
AND THE CUSTOMERS WE LOST

IF OUR FINANCIAL STATEMENTS
TURN OUT BAD (AS THEY HAVE SAID)
WE MAY NEED MEDICATION
THAT CAN HELP REMOVE THE RED

WE HOPE THIS ONE POOR QUARTER
ISN'T APT TO HAPPEN TWICE
AND FOR OUR SHARES OUTSTANDING
WON'T DEPRESS THE MARKET PRICE

WE'LL HAVE A GOOD DEDUCTION
FOR OUR INCOME TAX REPORT
BUT THAT'S THE ONLY BLESSING
THAT OUR ACTIONS WILL SUPPORT

Our Error Rate
Is 48(%)

WE STARTED NEW PRODUCTION
HOPING THAT IT WOULD ABATE
THE LOSS OF OUR CONSUMERS
BOTH AT HOME AND OUT OF STATE

WE TOLD ALL OF OUR SALES FOLKS
TO HAVE SAMPLES IN THEIR PACKS
AND HAND THEM OUT TO PEOPLE
JUST TO PROVE OUR TASTE WAS BACK

THIS CLIMBING BACK WAS PAINFUL
SINCE ITS PACE WAS RATHER SLOW
BUT WE HAD EXPECTATIONS
AND EXPERIENCE TO GROW

OUR OBJECTIVES WERE ACCOMPLISHED
AND WE'RE BACK ON EVEN KEEL
WITH PROFIT LEVELS HIGHER
AND SECURITY THAT'S REAL

WE'RE STILL EXPANSION-MINDED
AS GOOD MANAGEMENT SHOULD BE
BUT WALKING VERSUS RUNNING
WILL BE FAST ENOUGH FOR ME

A Steady Pace
Will Win the Race

OUR CONTRACTS WITH FRUIT GROWERS
HAD NO VOLUME DISCOUNT PLAN
AND PRICES WE WERE PAYING
WERE THE SAME SINCE WE BEGAN

WE TRIED NEGOTIATIONS
THAT WOULD RECOGNIZE OUR GROWTH
AND MAKE SOME CONTRACT CHANGES
THAT WOULD BENEFIT US BOTH

OUR ARGUMENTS AND TACTICS
HAD NO REAL EFFECT AT ALL
SINCE MOST OF THESE ORCHARD MERCHANTS
THOUGHT OUR BACK WAS TO THE WALL

BUT WE'D HAD FREQUENT PROBLEMS
GETTING CHERRIES SHIPPED IN TIME
TO MEET OUR BAKING SCHEDULES
WHICH CONTINUE IN THEIR CLIMB

AND OUR SUPPLY OF APPLES
HASN'T ALWAYS BEEN THE BEST
AND, FOR OUR TASTING STANDARDS,
HAVEN'T ALWAYS PASSED THE TEST

We Tend to Squirm
with Half a Worm

THIS LACK OF UNDERSTANDING
BY THE GROWERS WE HAD MET
MADE BUYERS QUITE FRUSTRATED
AND THE REST OF US UPSET

WE NEEDED DIFFERENT SOURCES
AND TO USE OUR COMMON SENSE
IN MAKING COST REDUCTIONS
IN OUR BASE INGREDIENTS

WE DID HAVE SOME INQUIRIES
FROM OUR SHAREHOLDERS AROUND
ON WHY WE WEREN'T PRODUCING
ALL OUR RAW STOCK FROM THE GROUND

SUCH VERTICAL EXPANSION
WOULD THEN SEEM TO LET US GROW
WITHOUT EXTREME DIVERSION
FROM THE PRODUCTS THAT WE KNOW

THEY SAID WE SHOULD OWN ORCHARDS
SO THAT WE COULD HAVE FIRST CALL
ON ALL THE FRUIT PRODUCTION
AND KEEP SHIPMENTS ON THE BALL

Early Firms
Get All the Worms

BECAUSE SOME ORCHARD SELLERS
MIGHT SUSPECT OUR FIRM WAS LARGE
WE USED AN OUTSIDE AGENT
TO PREVENT AN OVERCHARGE

                WE ASKED HIM TO START LOOKING
              FOR SOME ORCHARDS WE COULD BUY
                  INCLUDING ALL THE SOURCES
              OF OUR CURRENT FRUIT SUPPLY

FOR IF HE WAS SUCCESSFUL
AND HIS CLIENT WASN'T NAMED
THERE WOULD BE SOME SURPRISES
WHEN NEW OWNERS WERE PROCLAIMED

                HE SAID HE'D USE DISCRETION
                 BUT HE COULD NOT GUARANTEE
              THAT OUR NAME COULD STAY HIDDEN
                  WITH SO LARGE AN INDUSTRY

DURING FINAL PURCHASE ACTIONS
WE ANNOUNCED JUST WHO WE WERE
TO SHOCK THOSE STUBBORN GROWERS
WHO HAD THOUGHT THEIR RATES SECURE

A Fruit Punch
for That Whole Bunch

WE NOW OWN SEVERAL ORCHARDS
FOR THE GROWING OF OUR FRUIT
BUT KEPT THE FORMER OWNERS
'STEAD OF GIVING THEM THE BOOT

THE REASON FOR THIS ACTION
WAS THE NEED FOR GROWING SKILL
AND NONE OF OUR OWN PEOPLE
COULD BEGIN TO FILL THE BILL

WE TOLD THEM WHAT WE NEEDED
AND JUST WHEN TO SHIP THE FRUIT
AND LEFT THEM THERE TO MANAGE
ANY WAY THEY THOUGHT WOULD SUIT

THIS LACK OF CLOSE CONTROLLING
ADDS A RISK TO OPERATIONS
AND THOUGH WE WRITE THEIR PAYCHECKS
THEY MAY STILL TAKE LONG VACATIONS

THERE IS A FINAL TESTING
EVEN THOUGH IT MAY CAUSE WASTE
BY DETERMINING DELIVERIES
ARE ON TIME AND HAVE GOOD TASTE

A Final Proof
They Didn't Goof

EACH MONTHLY INCOME STATEMENT
SHOWS OUR FRUIT COSTS ARE REDUCING
AND PRODUCTS ARE THE VERY BEST
SINCE WE BEGAN PRODUCING

        OUR SHAREHOLDERS ARE HAPPY
        WITH OUR NEW EXPANSION ACTS
        AND WE'VE BEEN VERY CAREFUL
        TO ENSURE THEY HAVE THE FACTS

WITH SALES AND PROFITS GAINING
AND A CASH IMPROVEMENT TREND
OUR SHAREHOLDERS HAVE ASKED US
TO DECLARE A DIVIDEND

        OF COURSE THIS MAKES ME HAPPY
        SINCE I OWN THE CONTROLLING SHARE
        AND WITH THE ADDED MONEY
        I SHOULD BE A MILLIONAIRE

AND ALL OUR OWN FINE PEOPLE
CAN RELAX ON EASY STREET
WITH SALARIES AND OPTIONS
AND WITH JOBS THAT CAN'T BE BEAT

Our Lifestyle
Transposes from Moonlight
to Roses

ALTHOUGH I NOW HAVE MONEY
I'M NOT SURE JUST WHAT TO DO
EXCEPT I'M EATING BETTER
AND WEAR CLOTHING THAT LOOKS NEW

                    MY FRIENDS ARE ALL ADVISORS
              (AND THEIR NUMBER SEEMS TO GROW)
                  AND TELL ME WHAT I'M LACKING
                    JUST IN CASE I DIDN'T KNOW

I KNOW I'M TOO PLATONIC
SO I WELCOME THEIR ADVICE
ON HOW TO LOOK OFFICIAL
REGARDLESS OF THE PRICE

                    I MOVED INTO A PENTHOUSE
                    WITH AN UP-TO-DATE DÉCOR
              AND BOUGHT A YACHT (WITH CAPTAIN)
                FOR THOSE WEEKENDS OFF THE SHORE

IN SPITE OF THESE ADDITIONS
IT SEEMED HARD TO STAY AWAY
FROM THOSE OFFICIAL DUTIES
FOR WHICH I RECEIVED MY PAY

I Ought to Stay and Work for Pay

THE REST OF OUR OFFICIALS
KEPT INSISTING I HAVE FUN
AND ASSURED ME THAT THE BUSINESS
WOULD CONTINUE TO BE RUN

                I DID EXTEND MY WEEKENDS
          WHICH CUT DOWN MY WORKING TIME
       AND JOINED THE FUN AND GAMESTERS
       AND THE CROWDS WHO WINE AND DINE

BUT MANY AT OUR PARTIES
HAD JUST RECENTLY ACQUIRED
THE PILES OF TIME AND MONEY
THAT THIS LIVING HAS REQUIRED

        WE STILL FELT SOMEWHAT CLUMSY
      AT THOSE GAMES THAT PEOPLE PLAY
           AND SELDOM WERE RELAXING
        WHETHER IT WAS NIGHT OR DAY

I FOUND THAT ALL THIS PLAYING
MADE ME TIRED THROUGHOUT THE WEEK
AND IN REGARD TO BUSINESS
MADE MY OLD DECISIONS CREAK

The Wearing
of the Green

MY LIFESTYLE WAS IMPOSING
BUT THE COSTS INCREASED SO FAST
MY BANK ACCOUNT KEPT SHRINKING
AND I FEARED IT MIGHT NOT LAST

    THE COST OF MY ADDITIONS
    WAS A MINOR CASH OUTLAY
    COMPARED TO THE EXPENSES
    OF THOSE FOLKS WHO CAME TO STAY

I TRIED TO MAKE SOME CUTTING
IN THE SIZE OF CROWDS AROUND
BY SORTING OUT THE DRIFTERS
FROM THE REAL FRIENDS I HAD FOUND

    MY EFFORTS WEREN'T PRODUCTIVE
    EVEN THOUGH I TRIED MY BEST
    SINCE I COULD NOT DISTINGUISH
    ALL MY GOOD FRIENDS FROM THE REST

I FINALLY STOPPED MY SPENDING
AND LET PARTIES PASS ME BY
AND WATCHED THE CROWDS DEPARTING
SINCE THE MONEY WELL RAN DRY

A Cashless Society

I ALSO MADE REDUCTIONS
IN MY FOOD AND DRINK SUPPLIES
BUT MY REFRIGERATOR
STILL CONTAINS SOME APPLE PIES

MY PENTHOUSE IS STILL FURNISHED
FOR OFFICIAL RECOGNITION
AND I DRESS IN PROPER CLOTHING
THAT I KEEP IN GOOD CONDITION

MY OCEAN-GOING VESSEL
THAT I STILL WAS PAYING FOR
WAS TRADED FOR ANOTHER
THAT WAS POWERED BY AN OAR

MY STACKS OF MUSIC RECORDS
USED FOR DANCING IN THE HALL
WERE GIVEN TO MY NEIGHBORS
WHO HAD SURELY HEARD THEM ALL

I SOLD MY LONG BLACK LIMO
AND DECIDED WITH A SHRUG
I'D BE THE ONLY CHAIRMAN
IN A CHAUFFER-DRIVEN BUG

The Volks Is Waggin'

WITH ALL THIS COST REDUCTION
I WAS ALMOST IN THE BLACK
WHICH MADE MY SLEEPING BETTER
EVERY TIME I HIT THE SACK

THE BUSINESS WAS PROGRESSING
JUST AS WELL AS WE HAD PLANNED
WITH INTEGRATED FUNCTIONS
RUNNING SMOOTHLY AND WELL-PLANNED

WE ALL BEGAN RELAXING
AFTER HAVING SHOWN EMOTION
AND REACTING SO DIRECTLY
TO OUR RECENT GROWTH EXPLOSION

OUR PIES KEPT TASTING BETTER
AS NEW STANDARDS WERE ATTAINED
AND DELIVERIES WERE FASTER
SO MORE FRESHNESS WAS RETAINED

SINCE ALL SEEMED MILK AND HONEY
WITH NO PROBLEMS TO FORESEE
WE STARTED GROWING SOFTER
THAN A BUSINESS GROUP SHOULD BE

We Can't Be Soft and Stay Aloft

THEN OLD MOTHER NATURE
THREW A CURVE LIKE VIDA BLUE[2]
BY FREEZING ALL OUR ORCHARDS
JUST AS HARD AS SHE COULD DO

[2] VIDA BLUE WAS A FAMOUS BASEBALL PITCHER FOR THE
OAKLAND ATHLETICS AND HELPED THE TEAM WIN THREE
CONSECUTIVE WORLD CHAMPIONSHIPS IN 1972-1974.

A Blue Norther

OUR FRUIT SUPPLY DIMINISHED
AT A VERY RAPID PACE
WHICH CAUSED AS LARGE A PROBLEM
AS WE EVER THOUGHT WE'D FACE

    THE PLANT PRODUCTION WORKERS
    GREW MORE ANXIOUS EVERY NIGHT
    BECAUSE THEIR INVENTORIES
    WERE BECOMING VERY TIGHT

OUR SALESMEN BECAME WORRIED
HAVING FEWER PIES TO SELL
AND WHEN THEY SAW THEIR BUYERS
WISHED FOR SOMETHING GOOD TO TELL

    WE SEARCHED THE OPEN MARKET
    IN A PANIC FOR MORE STOCK
    BUT FOUND MOST OTHER ORCHARDS
    ALSO FROZEN LIKE A ROCK

WE HOPED THAT FOREIGN COUNTRIES
MIGHT HAVE ORCHARDS TO EXPLORE
BUT FOUND THEIR FRUIT PRODUCTION
WAS ALREADY SPOKEN FOR

We Might Need Soon to Search the Moon

OUR CASH POSITION SUFFERED
WITH OUR SALES BECOMING TOUGH
AND FOR INVENTORY STOCKING
WE JUST DIDN'T HAVE ENOUGH

WE CUT BACK ON THE PAYROLL
FOR OFFICIAL MANAGEMENT
AND DEVELOPED COST REDUCTIONS
BY CONTROLLING WHAT WE SPENT

WE USED OUR PENCILS LONGER
AND RECYCLED PAPER CLIPS
OUR MEMOS WERE HANDWRITTEN
AND WE PLANNED ON FEWER TRIPS

THE ENERGY REDUCTION
IN OUR LIGHTS AND POWER AND HEAT
WAS CONSISTENT WITH THE NATION
AND HELPED IN OUR COST RETREAT

I EVEN SOLD SOME ASSETS
AND LOANED PROCEEDS TO THE FIRM
BUT ALL THESE DESPERATE ACTIONS
ONLY COVERED A SHORT TERM

We Need Cash
to Stop a Crash

SINCE FUNDS WERE INSUFFICIENT
TO FULFILL PROSPECTIVE NEEDS
WE ARRANGED TO BORROW MONEY
IN AMOUNTS THE BANK AGREED

    AND NOW OUR PLANT AND ORCHARDS
    ARE ALL MORTGAGED TO THE TOP
    BUT CASH FLOW'S STILL DECREASING
    IN A TREND WE CANNOT STOP

WE HOPE THE CROP RENEWAL
WILL SOON TURN OUR LUCK AROUND
AND START THE BUSINESS CYCLE
THAT BEGINS WITH FERTILE GROUND

    THE BANKS HAVE SET UP SCHEDULES
    FOR REPAYMENT OF OUR DEBT
    BUT AS FOR MY CASH ADVANCES
    I WAS TOLD I SHOULD FORGET

I DON'T THINK OF THIS BADLY
SINCE THE ASSETS THAT I SOLD
WERE LUXURIES AND PLAYTHINGS
I'D FORGET AS I GROW OLD

I'll Just Be Glad for What I Had

THE VENTURE WILL RECOVER
(AT LEAST ALL OUR BANKERS SAY)
WITH NO MORE ANXIOUS MOMENTS
FOR OUR PEOPLE AND THEIR PAY

    OUR BUSINESS DOES SEEM BETTER
    EVEN THOUGH IT'S BUILDING SLOW
    SO ALL OF US ARE HOPEFUL
    THAT WE'RE REALLY ON THE GO

WE'VE REARRANGED OUR PEOPLE
SO THE YOUNG ONES COULD GROW TOO
AND RETIRED A FEW OLD TIMERS
WHO HAD PENSIONS COMING DUE

    THE REST WERE VERY THANKFUL
    THAT THEY HAD SURVIVED THE TEST
    AND HAVE SUFFICIENT STATURE
    TO REMAIN AMONG THE BEST

BECAUSE OF BEING FOUNDER
AND THE GRAY THAT'S IN MY HAIR
I'VE BEEN PROMOTED UPWARD
TO AN HONORARY CHAIR

A Padded Chair
for the Old Gray Mare

I FEEL JUST LIKE A FIXTURE
IN AN OAKEN OFFICE FRAME
ALTHOUGH I REALLY HAVEN'T
ANYONE THAT I COULD BLAME

        I'M TORN WITH INDECISION
      SINCE I STILL FEEL VERY GOOD
        AND COULD CONTINUE MAKING
      ALL DECISIONS THAT I SHOULD

BUT THEN I MUST REMEMBER
THAT I STARTED OUT FROM SCRATCH
AND WENT THROUGH ALL THE HEADACHES
THAT OUR GROWING PAINS COULD HATCH

      I HAVEN'T MUCH FOR SHOWING
      SINCE MY ASSETS ARE SO FEW
        BUT SHUDDER AT REPEATING
    ALL THE PANICS I'VE BEEN THROUGH

SO IN CONSIDERATION
OF THESE PAST AND FUTURE POINTS
I GUESS I'LL JUST BE GRACEFUL
AND RETIRE MY ACHING JOINTS

Reduced That Aching by Sun-Baking

THIS IDEA THAT RETIREMENT
IS AN IDEAL WAY TO GO
MAY WELL FIT FOR SOME PEOPLE
BUT FOR ME JUST ISN'T SO

                    I TRIED MY HAND AT FISHING
            WHICH I HAD TO LEARN FROM SCRATCH
                    BUT THEN I GAVE UP QUICKLY
            WHEN I COULDN'T LAND A CATCH

I WENT TO SEE THE MOVIES
BUT THEY SEEMED INVOLVED WITH SEX
AND MEMORY SADLY FAILED ME
WHEN I WATCHED THOSE RATED X

            THOSE LESSONS AT THE GOLF COURSE
                    WERE NOT REALLY VERY TOUGH
                    EXCEPT MY PROPER STROKING
                ALWAYS PUT ME IN THE ROUGH

I EVEN TRIED BIRD WATCHING
AND COLLECTING BUTTERFLIES
BUT ALL THIS MADE ME WONDER
IF RETIREMENT WAS SO WISE

I'll Wait to Share in Medicare

I FINALLY GOT THE COURAGE
TO ADMIT THAT I HAD FAILED
IN ADJUSTING TO RETIREMENT
AND THE FUN AND GAMES ENTAILED

MY NEXT STOP WAS THE OFFICE
WHERE I USED TO HANG MY HAT
I ASKED FOR AN APPOINTMENT
WITH THE MANAGEMENT AT BAT

I TOLD A FEW DIRECTORS
THAT MY PENSION WAS OK
BUT WANTED TO DO SOMETHING
TO HELP PASS THE TIME EACH DAY

THEY UNDERSTOOD MY PROBLEM
BUT HAD LITTLE THEY COULD DO
SINCE THEIR RETIREMENT LOGIC
WAS WHEN YOU'RE THROUGH YOU'RE THROUGH

I KNOW THEY WERE ASPIRING
TO HIGHER BUSINESS STAKES
SO I DECIDED I WOULD LET THEM
JUST REPEAT MY OLD MISTAKES

It's Their Turn for a Burn

I THEN MADE A SUGGESTION
THAT I THOUGHT WOULD CAUSE SOME SHOCK
TO TAKE MY PAY IN APPLES
FROM THEIR INVENTORY STOCK

I'M NOW BACK AT MY CORNER
SELLING APPLES ONE BY ONE
AND WATCHING OTHERS HUSTLE
WHILE RELAXING IN THE SUN

The Business Notion
Stops Its Motion

ABOUT THE AUTHOR

JIM WHITACRE was born on August 26, 1915 in Kensington, Ohio. He was the only child of Ralph and Lenah Whitacre. In 1917, the family moved to Kansas City, MO, where Jim excelled in school and graduated from business college in 1936 with a degree in accounting. Jim went to work for Arthur Anderson and continued taking accounting courses at night. He passed the CPA exam on his first try.

Jim and his wife Marion were married in 1939 and Jim traveled extensively on projects for Arthur Anderson. In 1957, he joined Collins Radio in Cedar Rapids, IA, as their general auditor. At the time, Collins Radio was a pioneer in satellite technology and supplied radio communication equipment to NASA for the Mercury, Gemini, and Apollo programs in the 1960s.

In 1963, Jim was transferred to Richardson, TX, where he continued as the senior internal auditor for Collins Radio. The company's first mainframe digital computer was installed at the Richardson facility and Jim utilized it to create accounting and auditing programs.

In the early 1970s, Jim was an established senior CPA and he turned his attention toward helping young accountants entering the business world for the first time. The young recruits were sharp with accounting skills but totally green in the ways of business. Jim had an idea to write a poem about starting a business and the various challenges a young entrepreneur might encounter. That idea was the origin of this book.

Jim Whitacre passed away much too early in 1985 at the age of 69.

www.ingramcontent.com/pod-product-compliance
Lightning Source LLC
Chambersburg PA
CBHW060748100426
42813CB00004B/742